A Matter of Life and Death

JOHN V. TAYLOR

A Matter of Life and Death

SCM PRESS LTD

© John V. Taylor 1986

British Library Cataloguing in Publication Data

Taylor, John V.
A matter of life and death.
1. Faith
I. Title
201   BT771.2

ISBN 0-334-00977-4

First published 1986 by
SCM Press Ltd
26–30 Tottenham Road London N1 4BZ
Third impression 1987

Typeset by Gloucester Typesetting Services,
and printed in Great Britain by
Richard Clay Ltd., Bungay, Suffolk

CONTENTS

PREFACE

This book consists of the five addresses given on consecutive evenings in the Sheldonian Theatre at Oxford during the Mission to the University in February 1986. Apart from a few attempts to improve the clarity of a statement, I have made only those changes that were needed to put the addresses in book form. In a few passages I have used or developed something I have written elsewhere, notably in the small book of meditations, *Weep not for me*, published by the World Council of Churches, whom I thank for giving me the freedom to do so.

I wish to thank Dr Anthony Phillips and the members of the Mission Committee for inviting me to do this work and for giving much valuable advice; and also Dr Kathleen Hall, recently retired from Southampton University, for undertaking the typing.

It was my wife who first discovered and then took me to see Ria Bancroft's bronze tabernacle doors in the Cathedral of the Blessed Sacrament at Christchurch, New Zealand, and I am very grateful to that artist and to the cathedral authorities for permission to use the photograph first on the posters advertising the Mission, and now on the cover of this book.

1

Breath of Life

By way of introducing both my subject and myself I want to start by telling briefly how a book came to be written.[1] In 1966 the Senate and Council of Birmingham University invited me to give the eight Edward Cadbury Lectures in Theology early in the following year. At that time I was kept very busy as the General Secretary of the Church Missionary Society and felt rather at a loss to know what I should talk about with little time to undertake fresh reading. I consulted my predecessor at the CMS, Max Warren, who was my most trusted spiritual guru, and he suggested some lecture titles under the general heading of 'The Holy Spirit and the Christian Mission'.

This appealed to me because I had already given a series of addresses on the Holy Spirit in several retreats, and was at that time intrigued by the theory that the Christian church had previously passed through two distinct phases in which its thought and devotion had been focussed successively on God the Father and then on Christ, and that we were now entering the era of the Holy Spirit. It also seemed to me that a clearer understanding of the Holy Spirit could help Christians to grapple with the question of the other great faiths in the world, which was obviously going to be the major theological issue for the rest of this century. Finally, as I settled down to prepare my material, I found myself enjoying it as a kind of personal salute to a former tutor and very dear friend who had recently died, Joe Fison, the Bishop of Salisbury, from whose writings about the Holy Spirit I was drawing substantially. As it turned out, his was the first of three deaths that put their mark on the book.

Well, the lectures were written and delivered and, according to the contract, I was supposed to get them published. But I was not satisfied. I asked for time to revise and improve, yet as I did so it was borne in on me that something was missing, something that should have been the key to the whole thing. I had written Hamlet without the Prince, and I had no idea what else there was to say.

Then someone else died. A woman I had known long before, but not much since, took her own life. It affected me more deeply than I realized. My wife noticed symptoms of anxiety that I was unaware of and very wisely and gently got me to a psychotherapist. I only had about two sessions, but they seemed to unlock something, for I couldn't stop talking when I got home.

Some time after that I was returning by train from Oxford to London on a late summer evening. My mind wandered from my paperback to the stubble fields where the stooks of corn cast long blue shadows towards the glowing trees. As so often before, I was moved and held by the beauty of it, and I began to think about what actually happens when a landscape or a great tree or the spectacle of the night sky presents itself and commands attention. That quite ordinary scene beyond the railway track had ceased to be merely an object I was looking at. It had become a subject imbued with a power that was affecting me, saying something to me in the way that music does. Something had generated a current of charged intensity between it and me. If I said that the significance and value that it had taken on was all a projection of my imagination, I knew that that would be understating the truth. In all such experiences a kind of mutual communication or exchange was taking place which did not originate entirely in myself. I was also quite sure that this was a very ordinary, almost universal human experience. I was not an animist, so I did not credit the corn stooks with consciousness. Then what was the source of this current of communication that makes a landscape or a person or an idea act upon me, or upon you, in this way? Who effects the introduction between me and that which is there, turning it into a presence towards which I surrender myself?

As soon as the question took that form the answer fell into place. So *this* is what is meant by the Holy Spirit! This is the essential nature of his power. This is why he is the universal Spirit of God, leaving no individual and no culture without his witness and challenge. This is how God acts upon human beings, maybe upon all created things, working from within, making them more aware.

I had been given the missing key to what I had been trying to write. New facets of this insight tumbled into my mind, and the last blank pages of my paperback were crammed with scribbled notes by the time I reached Paddington. I remembered not only other occasions when beauty in one form or another had 'spoken' to me, but also a moment during one of those hated maths periods at school when weeks of humiliating blindness and boredom fell away in a flash of comprehension.

That 'I see it now!' is the classical response to the action of the Holy Spirit who is the anonymous opener of our eyes. I recalled a student from an Afrikaans background in South Africa who was staying with us one Christmas time when we lived in Uganda. As we returned from a party the Bishop had given he was silent, but before we went to our beds he described how he had been standing alone in a side room during the party when a black child and a white had run in, hand in hand, stopped to whisper like conspirators, and run out again, laughing. Something so normal, yet at that moment it had struck him like a portent and he felt his whole world turn over. He was already calculating what it would mean to return to his country so changed. Whether the thing we see in this new way is religious and moral or something quite different is not the point. The Spirit of God is at work to bring us to life, to make us more awake and aware, and so lead us to fresh discovery and a fresh response. He helps us to make the connection by opening the doors of perception, generating a current of communication, opening the eyes. There is nothing in this earth more powerful or more revolutionary than a newly recognized idea, or a situation seen in a new way. This is why the Christian church, for all its institutional lethargy and its sorry concern for its own interests, continues to throw up men and women who have seen an area of need, unrecognized before, or an injustice that none have challenged, and who will not be silenced.

For the first time I realized why that familiar Christian prayer which we call 'The Grace' runs the way it does. It fastens on the most characteristic attributes of God the Father, of Jesus Christ and of the Holy Spirit. So it speaks of the grace or given-ness of Jesus Christ, the love of God, and then, not

4

the power of the Holy Spirit, as many would expect, nor his light and guidance, but the *communion*, the communication, of the Holy Spirit. And again in that list of his gifts which Christian prayers have quoted from the Old Testament, the quality that predominates is perception: 'the Spirit of wisdom and understanding, counsel, knowledge' (Isa. 11.2).

For the next few weeks after that train journey my thoughts continued to flow in full spate so that I had little time to compare notes and discover others who might have already enlarged upon this idea that had newly come to me. Before I had begun to look further afield a third death occurred, this time of an older friend, Dr James Welsh, one-time head of the Religious Broadcasting Department at the BBC, who had more recently been a lecturer in philosophy at the University of Surrey. At his memorial service I heard a reading from the Jewish philosopher, Martin Buber's little book, *I and Thou*, which, to my shame, I had not come across till then. It spoke to me as a strong confirmation that I was on the right track, even though it did not mention the Holy Spirit by name.

To man the world is two-fold, in accordance with his two-fold attitude. He perceives what exists around him – simply things, and beings as things . . . It is to some extent a reliable world . . . It is your object . . . You cannot hold on to life without it; its reliability sustains you; but should you die in it your grave would be in nothingness.

Or, on the other hand man meets what exists and becomes as what is over against him . . . Between you and it there is a mutual giving: you say *Thou* to it and give yourself to it, it says *Thou* to you and gives itself to you. You cannot make yourself understood with others concerning it, you are

5

alone with it . . . It does not help to sustain you in life, it only helps you to glimpse eternity.[2]

The drawback in that exceptionally beautiful passage is that, by generalizing, Buber makes it sound as though the seeing of something else as a 'Thou' is a rare and mystical experience. By talking about the view from a train or a moment in a school classroom I am trying to insist that the 'opening of the eyes' is given in the most ordinary ways and to most ordinary people, and, as I have said, it is not necessarily realized as a 'religious' experience at all.

One of the best known examples of this is the incident that led Sir Alexander Fleming to the identification of penicillin. André Maurois' biography of Fleming describes how, as early as 1922, a chance observation led him to the discovery that an enzyme secreted in the more exposed tissues of plants and animals had the power of dissolving many types of microbe; but he could find no way of inoculating human subjects safely with enough of the enzyme to combat the most dangerous bacteria. Six years later he was still searching for a general antiseptic capable of killing bacteria in the human bloodstream without destroying human cells in the process. He had temporarily interrupted his work in order to write an article for a younger colleague on the staphylococci microbes, and he sat in his little laboratory surrounded by innumerable culture dishes in apparent disorder. In them the colonies of staphylococci were cultivated on agar, and Fleming had to remove the lids while he examined the contents under the microscope. The colleague for whom he was doing this work dropped in to talk. Fleming, grumbling at the ease with which foreign bodies contaminated the culture dishes, picked up several of them to throw them away. 'Suddenly,' writes Maurois, 'he stopped talking, then, after a moment's observation, said in his usual unconcerned tones: "That's funny . . ." On the culture at which he was looking there was a growth of mould, as on several of the others, but on this particular one, all round the mould, the colonies of staphylococci had been dissolved, and . . . looked like drops of dew.'[3] Fleming kept that Petri dish for the rest of his life. By chance the spores of a rare mould had been blown in through the open window from Praed Street; but it was the sudden gift of 'seeing the ordinary in a new way' which enabled Fleming to give penicillin to the world.

It is exactly the same gift which in a more domestic context enables people who are very close to each other to communicate without blundering. Words may not be the best way. One or the other may be bad at words. But the parent whose ear or eye is quick with recognition will notice the well-concealed distress of a child who has had a bad experience at school, and know how to relieve the hurt with tact; and the man or woman in whom the gift of awareness is at work will pick up the partner's tentative, unspoken signals of affection and support. The opposite experience is sadly more common. We miss the point of the message or fail to hear the cry and trample on each other with ludicrous clumsiness. Or, all too often, we were, in fact, aware but would not *let* ourselves understand. So the unspoken exchange that could have taken place was cut off. We are responsible for most of our own blindness and deafness. Yet the Spirit of God goes on renewing the gift.

The Religious Experience Research Unit based in Oxford has collected a great number of accounts of just such a lighting up of awareness as I have been describing. Typical of many of them is an occasion recalled by a man in his mid-fifties who said in an interview:

I think perhaps I was six. I was taken to a park in the evening to enjoy a firework display. It was summer. There was a crowd of people by the lake . . . Against the darkening sky, before the fireworks were set alight, I remember seeing these trees, poplar trees they were, three of them. It's very difficult to say exactly what happened because the order of this experience is of its own kind. There was a breeze and the leaves of the poplars vibrated, rustled. I believe I said to myself, 'How beautiful, how wonderful those three trees are.' I think there was awe and wonder, and I remember comparing the luminousness – that's a grown-up word, of course – the marvellous beauty, the haunting oppressive power of those trees with the artificiality of the surroundings, the people, the fireworks and so on. Oddly, I kind of knew that this was something extraordinary at the moment it occurred. It was as simple as that, just seeing these trees, but it was the event of my childhood . . . I knew then it was going to last. And so it has . . . What happened was telling me something. But what was it telling? The fact of divinity, that it was good? – not so much in the moral sense, but that it was beautiful, yes, sacred.[4]

On the face of it this was an early aesthetic experience, a waking up to natural beauty, with no distinct religious content. Yet to the man himself it affirmed divinity, made it sure. I find this a fascinating characteristic of all these occasions of enhanced awareness: the conventional definitions of what is religious and what is not fall away. As a woman's letter in the

8

archives of the Religious Experience Research Unit puts it, 'I am convinced that meeting with "God" is not a religious experience but, rather, a real-life experience.' That is profoundly true, and it is bound to be so because in every 'opening of the eyes', every encounter with the greater reality, God is not to be found in the thing that is seen but in the *seeing*, for he is the source and giver of that kind of seeing. This, I think, is the significance of the well-known incident in the Old Testament when Moses, the fugitive from the tyrant King of Egypt, herding sheep in the Sinai peninsular, sees a shrub that is on fire yet, strangely, not burnt up. Did it 'strike' him then as an image of his people's long torment in the furnace of Egyptian oppression? At any rate he was overwhelmed by the sense of the presence of God, not so much in the bush as in the seeing. The same is true of the experience of another fugitive, the prophet Elijah. Seeking a fresh confirmation of God's reality, he was given on the bare mountainside a vivid encounter with hurricane, earthquake and fire. Yet it was not in these that he found God but in the communication, the still small voice, that awoke him to the significance of things.[5] This is why it is a complete misunderstanding to dismiss any of the experiences I have recounted as 'nature worship'. Wordsworth was not worshipping nature. The particular object or idea of which we become so intensely aware does not ultimately matter. It may have been a religious picture or a cluster of trees, a philosophical concept or a laboratory specimen. The essential element in all these experiences is the gift of awareness, the 'coming alive'.

This is made beautifully clear in a philosophy student's account of a mental jump which took him by surprise over lunch one day.

I had become increasingly worried by the apparently inevitable conclusion that if God did not exist it seemed impossible to provide any rational basis for those values which I wanted to adopt. Increasingly life seemed to be meaningless. Why, if there is no God, should anything exist in the first place? Indeed, how could anything exist? Why not just nothing? At this point in my reasoning it was as if suddenly a door had been opened in the mind which it is difficult to find language to describe . . . It was like an intuition of infinity and pure reason. I had caught sight of the truth which the human faculties in their frailty are unable to grasp; and if I could not understand those mysteries, at least I could know that there is something beyond, and I could have faith in the existence of God. Then the door was closed quietly and the vision slipped away like a dream . . . I continued with my meal and my cabbage, boiled as only the English know how.[6]

That story reminds me of the exasperating conclusion to the Book of Job which seems to offer no answer to the problem of undeserved suffering yet leaves the sufferer himself answered. So for this young philosopher the reality of God was encountered, not at the end of a train of thought, but in the opening of a door into a different kind of knowing.

To sum up, then, I would say that God the Spirit is the unceasing animator and communicator, the inexhaustible source of insight, awareness, recognition and response. He is the awakener, and that is how he works upon us. The Christian Creed calls this Spirit 'The Lord, the Giver of Life', and it is this 'coming to life' which is being denoted in that poetical imagery at the beginning of the Bible of the Creator breathing the breath of life into the nostrils of the new-made human creature so that it became a living soul.

But that awakening of awareness and response in the human species has been only the culmination of an unimaginably long creative process which can properly be described as a stirring of all things into movement towards greater complexity and interaction, towards an extended awareness and response. Development could equally be regressive; it was not automatically 'upward'; yet, as the options increased so, it seems, did the pull of an unrealized potential. There was a thrust towards more sensitivity and mutuality, the beginnings of a nervous system, the successive dawn of perception, of consciousness, of communication, of thought. Unless the whole direction has changed we must judge that whatever tends to make us yet more aware, more responsive and responsible, more fully alive, is on the side of creativity. And every refusal to respond, every evasion of awareness, every choice that deadens, even though it be done in the name of progress or in the name of religion, is a tiny step towards regression. Which is only another way of saying that the Holy Spirit, who is the Creator Spirit, the Lord and Giver of Life, has always been quietly, anonymously at work within every human life, within me, within you, drawing your attention to this, to that, opening your eyes, making you aware, awakening all that is truly human in you, all that is most real. Without fully realizing it you have often resisted him, finding it too painful to be made fully alive, more comfortable to be a bit insensitive, a bit dead. There have been times when you were stirred with the excitement of a new project, a different interest, an issue of justice that called for support, but it was too much trouble to make room for it. Times, perhaps, when you saw yourself more clearly, knew what you needed to do, but found it too disturbing to pursue. Moments when something strangely beautiful claimed your attention, demanded that you stand and stare, but it was too embarrassing in front of your friends. And when, unexpectedly, God has become more possible, more real, you couldn't let yourself stay with it. These experiences are common to every life, whether they have taken a religious form or not. Thank God that his Spirit is not easily rebuffed, for it is the Spirit of love. It is the Spirit of life, striving with our dull, frightened little spirits to bring us fully to life. He has more to give us than the occasional prompting, more than those rare moments of 'seeing in a new way'. Those are hints of a more permanent aliveness to which the Holy Spirit can bring a human being.

Does that sound fanciful, too much to hope for? Well, as we grow up we become sceptical towards the fairy tales of childhood and ask with Nicodemus in the gospel, 'How can anyone be brought to life halfway through his lifetime? How can a man be born again when he is old?' And Jesus Christ, who was himself the totally alive human being, totally animated by the Holy Spirit of God, answered him as one who knew: 'If a man is not born of water and the Spirit he cannot enter the kingdom of God' (John 3.4–5).

That kingdom of right relationships is the true homeland of the fully alive, and it is the action of the Holy Spirit that brought them to life and keeps them alive. I am not talking about some abnormal religious state, though we shouldn't expect the energizer of life itself to be bound by our ideas of decorum. But the essential gift of the new truth is aliveness – coming alive towards other people, coming alive to the glory and tragedy of this world, coming alive towards the reality of ourselves, coming alive to our responsibility in society, local and worldwide; above all, coming alive towards the scriptures and the life of prayer, alive to the presence of Jesus Christ and the vast, embracing joy of God.

It is the gift of the Holy Spirit and, as I have said, every person has received premonitions and foretastes of different kinds. We cannot switch it on, this new aliveness, just because we feel ready for it. The Spirit is as free and unpredictable as the wind which blows where it wills. You simply ask for it; ask and wait trustfully; and let yourself come alive. Have the courage to lower the barriers, and welcome life. 'Ye that seek after God, *let* your heart live' (Ps. 63.32).

Spirit of God,
Lord and Giver of Life,
moving between us and around,
like wind or water or fire;
breathe into us your freshness that we may awake;
cleanse our vision that we may see more clearly;
kindle our senses that we may feel more sharply;
and give us the courage to live
as you would have us live,
through Jesus Christ our Lord.
Amen.

2

More Dead than Alive

If you pick up an old brown tennis ball from the long grass and in the palm of your hand it wriggles, you drop it quick. When you see it is only the children's hamster on the loose again your alarm seems ridiculous. But at the moment of contact when you realized 'It's alive!' your reaction was prompt – and so was the hamster's.

The essence of that vitality which makes a person or a family or a community really alive is responsiveness, or ability to respond. Even at the simple biological level this is true. When I had an operation last November under a local anaesthetic, the anaesthetist went over the skin of my thighs and stomach, pricking with a needle to test whether the injection had worked, and I was thankful that there was no response whatever. My capacity for feeling was dead. But on other occasions I am pleased when the doctor's little hammer, tapping that nerve below the kneecap to test my reactions, produces a healthy kick. Then I know there's life in me yet.

Many a child visiting Madame Tussaud's waxworks has discovered whether the attendant at the foot of the stairs was alive or not only by asking him a question or poking him in the ribs. Response or non-response is the test.

But this is even more true as a test of the quality or intensity of life in a person or a family or a community. We all know the difference between the person who is immediately interested in one on all occasions and aware of what one is trying to say and another person who seems never to be totally there and makes one feel diminished and constrained. We know the difference between the family that may be disorderly, feckless and unpredictable yet can be relied on in one particular, their atmosphere of liveliness, affection and welcome, and the family whose members may be far more accomplished, philanthropic and correct, yet remain withdrawn and unshared. And some of you must have experienced the contrast between a local community which made you feel at the same time both regimented and ignored, and some other community which gave you the sense of being much more yourself while sharing in something bigger than yourself. This is what I mean by life, or the lack of life, and the determining factor is awareness and the exchange of responses.

It has long been my conviction that God is not hugely concerned as to whether we are religious or not. What matters to God, and matters supremely, is whether we are alive or not. If your religion brings you more fully to life, God will be in it; but if your religion inhibits your capacity for life or makes you run away from it, you may be sure God is against it, just as Jesus was.

The Book of Deuteronomy in chapters 27–30 preserves the tradition that Moses before his death had drawn up the form of a simple ceremony whereby the Israelite tribes were to renew their allegiance to God after their conquest and occupation of Palestine. They were to muster on the main pass across the central mountain range where it was guarded by the ancient fortress of Shechem. Half the people were to be drawn up on the hill to the north of the valley and half on the south while the ministers of God's law intoned the solemn blessings that would reward their obedience and the curses that would light upon their neglect. But in the final analysis the choice before them was to be a simple matter of life and death, so simple that even the most religiously uninformed, the most earthy among them, could grasp what was at stake. I quote:

> The commandment that I lay on you this day is not too difficult for you, it is not too remote. It is not in heaven, that you should say, 'Who will go up to heaven for us to fetch it and tell it to us so that we can keep it?' Nor is it beyond the sea (some esoteric foreign cult) that you should say, 'Who will cross the sea for us to fetch it and tell it to us so that we can keep it?' It is a thing very near to you, upon your lips (something in common parlance) and in your heart (a universal human quest) ready to be kept. Today I offer you the choice of life and death, blessing or curse. Choose life (Deut. 30.11–15, 19, 20).

The issue couldn't be more recognizable or more familiar: Are you alive or dead? Is our community alive or dead? Choose life!

Well, who wouldn't? If choice comes into it, if the quality of our living and the level of our personal awareness is not already written on the cards of our glands or our genes, but lies to some extent in our own hands, then why, in God's name, are so many people only half alive? Why is it such a commonplace that little children are more vividly alive than their parents? Or why should the young express so great a dread of becoming middle-aged?

A young married man who worked at Heathrow Airport told me once how he and his wife had taken their two children for a day at the seaside. Their little boy of eighteen months needed the public toilet and the father set out with him to cross the rough unmetalled road above the beach. The expedition lasted all of half an hour, he told me, because every pebble, every bit of shell, every dry twig on the surface of that road was an object of such wonder that they had to squat and examine and exclaim. Heaven lies about us in our infancy and even a visit to the loo can become the golden journey to Samarkand. Where did it go, that intensity of response? How comes it that most of us lose the gift of seeing the ordinary as extraordinary? This is why Jesus Christ said that the kingdom of God is for the childlike, for it is the kingdom of the fully alive. The unaware and the half-dead have no place in it because they have no feeling for it.

There is a frightening amount of deadness around in our Western societies these days. It has not always been so. In other periods there has been abundant vigour, and the predominant malaise was of a different sort – ingrained enmity between families and tribes at one time; avarice and heartless exploitation at another. For there is a variety of deadly sins, just as there is a variety of plagues, and, like the several plagues, they do not offer the luxury of choosing which we will have, but now one, now another, falls upon the whole community, infecting the atmosphere that we all breathe. Of those so-called deadly sins, the more virulent epidemics of the human spirit, the one that has gripped our society in this century is, without question, *accidie*, the sleeping sickness, which is not so much sloth as we understand it, as apathy, lack of response, the total antithesis of that aliveness and awareness which is my theme in this book. And if there is salvation as the Christian gospel claims, it has to come to us as the remedy for this particular scourge and bring the half-dead to life. But first we must get the diagnosis right.

This inner lifelessness is induced by fear. People shrink from the pain of being fully awake. The child who is so intensely alive to the wonder of each shell and pebble quickly discovers that he cannot tunnel that vision so as to be aware of the beautiful and happy things alone. Eyes that remain open to the glory of the world must see its ugliness as well. The exchange between living beings on which life depends must include bad things as well as good. Those who respond to the 'otherness' of other people and, in Shakespeare's phrase, take upon themselves the mystery of things, will respond with the same sensitivity to other people's mess and muddle and take upon themselves their pain and anger. Buddhists preserve the tradition that Prince Sakyamuni was guarded by his royal parents from all contact with poverty, disease and death and even from the knowledge of their existence. When the inevitable happened, and in one day he encountered all three, the discovery was devastating. Thenceforth he set himself to liberate his mind from every vestige of evasion and illusion and so attained to Buddhahood or Enlightenment.

It does involve great pain and takes enormous courage to remain fully exposed and receptive towards the reality of the world around, towards the reality of the human beings we know, towards the reality of our own selves, towards the ultimate reality beyond and within all this. It also, incidentally, brings upon us a great deal of trouble and effort, since an ability to respond makes us take responsibility, and a readiness to answer makes us answerable. Consequently, and understandably, our growing up is usually a process of closing up. We actually choose to be less alive in order to be less bothered. So in that sense the word *accidie* does mean a deadly kind of laziness or sloth. Awareness makes demands, awareness hurts, so we begin to grow a protective shell and become a little blind, a little deaf, a little dead. That is what characterized the Priest and the Levite in the parable of Jesus about the traveller who fell among thieves. They passed by without apparently noticing the victim at the side of the road. Over the years those professionally religious men had trained themselves *not* to notice. The next one to come down the road, however, had kept his awareness painfully, responsibly alive. That is what turns a stranger into a neighbour. The chorus of women of Canterbury in T. S. Eliot's *Murder in the Cathedral* speaks for all of us who are plagued by apathy, including many who are still young.

> We do not wish anything to happen.
> Seven years we have lived quietly,
> Succeeded in avoiding notice,
> Living and partly living.
> There have been oppression and luxury,
> There have been poverty and licence,
> There has been minor injustice.
> Yet we have gone on living,
> Living and partly living.[1]

Quietly avoiding notice, and quietly avoiding having to take notice, is a recipe for making an irresponsible community in which nobody matters because nobody cares. So we invest all our expectations of a warm, living relationship in a partnership of a man and a woman. They start with an intense awareness and openness towards each other, but they find that the demands of that awareness and the embarrassment of that openness are too much for the immature and unresolved parts of themselves to sustain. So they learn to become a little more blind and deaf and dumb until communication breaks down, usually long before any serious unfaithfulness has taken place. The death of a marriage, which is now a legally recognized condition, is only another tragic casualty of that epidemic lifelessness, induced by fear, which is plaguing us at so many levels of experience.

The same deadness as afflicts our personal life also grips the institutions of power and decision-making, sapping the political will. Energies are channelled into the conflict of parties and ideologies rather than the business of getting things done. The violent posturing, the awful jargon of denigration, the masquerade of debate and conference long after decisions have been taken by quite different people – these are like the reflexes of something that has already died, while 'the common people' are everywhere paralysed by their frustration over the ineffectiveness of it all in the face of our global needs and fears. Things have grown worse rather than better since Eliot wrote in 1925, at a time when, in his own words, he had 'gone dead':

> We are the hollow men
> We are the stuffed men
> Leaning together
> Headpiece filled with straw. Alas!
> Our dried voices, when

23

> We whisper together
> Are quiet and meaningless
> As wind in dry grass.[2]

This widespread malaise has much in common with patho-
logical depression. The sufferers from that mental sickness
feel they are only half alive, drained of energy and hope. The
tragic multiplication of these sufferers in our day may be
related to the more general lifelessness that I am talking about,
but their deadness and despair is compounded by a sense of
worthlessness and self-punishment generated from the un-
bearable ambiguity of a childhood hatred towards someone
who was also loved, usually a parent. The skills of a doctor
and a psychoanalyst are necessary to the restoration of such
people to fullness of life, and if ever I have been called upon to
help one of them it has always been in collaboration with
those other practitioners. What I am concerned with in this
chapter is the more general drift towards an unwitting choice
of deadness rather than aliveness, and that is a *spiritual* sickness. It is described – diagnosed, you might say – in a vivid
series of phrases in the New Testament Letter to the Ephesians.
'They live in the emptiness of their minds, their wits darkened,
being estranged from the life which is in God through the
incomprehension that is in them through the stony hardness of
their hearts. They are those who have ceased to feel' (4.17–19).

Those who choose to grow the protective shell because it
is safer and more comfortable that way are not for the most
part aware of their deadness, since awareness is the faculty
they have anaesthetized. Something is missing, however, and
they try in various ways to whip up the lost exhilaration and
fend off the encroaching boredom. There are many sorts of

24

experience that momentarily reproduce a sense of vivid life and that dissolving of boundaries by which one becomes part of the unity of things. Drugs will do this for you while they last but they let you down into a more horrible lifelessness each time. A flaming row can bring one dramatically to life for a while, and so can many other 'performances'; which is what drives the raconteur to dominate the dinner table. Yet even while the squabble or the long story is in full spate the speaker's eyes betray the knowledge that in another moment he is going to feel deflated again. Others use sex as a way of capturing the sense of aliveness and the disappearance of boundaries, but unless it leads steadily into a fuller commitment, it becomes an increasingly self-absorbed search for an illusory coming to life which cannot add any meaning to the rest of life, as genuine experiences of awareness do.

These sad simulations of life by those who shrink from the cost of being really alive lay claim to a virility they do not actually possess. They masquerade as something full-blooded or even reckless, and this is a lie that has taken in the moralists of all periods. The fact is that addiction and promiscuity and violence are all manifestations of emptiness and what they confer is boredom.

> Those who have crossed
> With direct eyes, to death's other Kingdom
> Remember us – if at all – not as lost
> Violent souls, but only
> As the hollow men
> The stuffed men . . .[3]

There are other more respectable ways by which those who are partly living simulate an aliveness and a real identity, and because they are more socially acceptable they are more deceptive and deadly. The oldest delusion of all is that life consists of achievement. The consumer society is built upon that lie. When a man or a woman has been badly put down or treated as a nobody the commonest antidote is a spending spree. Like addicts, people crave for more possessions or higher attainments or new experiences to offset the emptiness and lack of selfhood. They sacrifice their children to the same craving, projecting upon them the hunger of their ambitions. Often they end by losing whatever real self they once had under a pile of achievements or of failures. Jesus Christ asked: 'What will it profit people, what will anyone make on the deal, if they gain the whole world and lose their own selves? What can be given to buy back life, aliveness?' (Mark 8.36, 37).

There is a typically religious version of this delusion of gaining life through achievement, namely, gaining life through rectitude. We Christians have talked rather a lot about keeping the rules. We have argued, reasonably enough on the face of it, that because the momentary boost of drugs or sex or violent rage or a new acquisition or a fresh attainment is no substitute for being really alive, then real life is to be gained by refraining from all those things and a lot besides. Of course we also recognized that good behaviour included a great many positive activities and attitudes and that those were even more important. Nevertheless we have tended to identify aliveness with what we call 'living a good life'. But this whole position collapses every time we meet the contrast between the two kinds of family which I drew earlier in this chapter – the well-mannered socially-acceptable family in which one can never quite be oneself and the uncouth, irregular lot who exude warmth and reality. Then it becomes glaringly obvious that keeping the rules cannot be a substitute for that life which the Lord God sets before us and urges us to choose.

This is what the apostle Paul was so often going on about in his epistles to the newly-formed churches. Their background and his was the practice of Judaism, even though more and more new Christians had not come from that tradition. The meticulous regulations governing every activity of the daily life of observing Jews are tiny reminders of God planted along the way to keep awareness and responsiveness fresh. But if observance is turned into another form of achievement as a substitute for real aliveness, then it becomes part of the structure of self-delusion and deadness. Paul had been caught in that trap in his own earlier life, so he argued vehemently against the notion that right behaviour is the way to become fully alive. 'If a law had been given which had power to bestow life,' he writes, 'then indeed a right relation would have come from keeping the law' (Gal. 3.21).

Clearly the writers of the New Testament knew about this deadness of spirit that I have been describing. They observed the processes by which it established itself in an individual or a community, very much as we might observe a disease. For example, they noted the interplay between the fear of life and the fear of death. You might have thought that people who have shrunk from the pain and the responsibility of being fully aware and awake, preferring the torpor of the partly living, would be fairly indifferent towards the eventual loss of something they have valued so little. But the opposite is the case. The thought of dying is most horrifying to those who have never fully lived. What makes people struggle so desperately against the certainty of becoming nothing is their failure ever to have been *anything*. That is why the literature of this century of the half-alive is haunted by the dread of not being any more. 'I'm going to die,' cries Pizarro in Shaffer's *Royal Hunt of the Sun*, 'and the thought of that dark has for years rotted everything for me, all simple joy in life.'[4] The significance of that admission lies in the fact that Pizarro, driven by the spectre of his own mortality, had destroyed the civilization of the Incas. Does this throw a new light on the nuclear threat in our own day, I wonder? On the other hand, those who welcome life with all its ambiguity and are kept open to the flow and exchange of that life, seem able to come to terms with their mortality almost as a matter of small account. There is a lovely example of this in a prayer composed by an Oxford undergraduate a few days after the outbreak of the First World War in which he was to be killed three years later. It runs:

> To have given me self-consciousness but for an hour in a world so breathless with beauty would have been enough. But thou hast preserved it within me for twenty years now and more, and hast crowned it with the joy of this summer of summers. And so, come what may, whether life or death, and, if death, whether bliss unimaginable or nothingness, I thank thee and bless thy name.[5]

That is very like the faith of the Old Testament in which, though for most of those past centuries the Hebrew people had no clear expectations of survival after death, their joy in the goodness of God while life lasted was ground enough for trust and praise. Christians see life in the light of the resurrection and believe that death is not the end of their relationship with God. But I think we get our emphasis wrong unless it can be summed up in the words: 'All this! – and heaven too.' That is far removed from the 'vale-of-tears' theology. It does more justice to the glory and the grief and the struggle of this world in which, if we will only open ourselves to receive it from God, we are already part of eternity.

But we don't, do we? We don't open ourselves to receive the many-splendoured richness of experience which is God's gift to us, and for which he has lifted us up through millions of years of development into sensitivity and response and the capacity for compassion and love and prayer. Seen in those terms the epidemic deadness I have tried to diagnose is a falling away from the divine design and a rejection of God's supreme invitation. It is *sin*, like that of the people in the parable of Jesus who found every possible excuse for staying away from the banquet of life.

Sin and death, deadness and sin, are bracketted together all through the Bible, not from the crude idea that our mortality is a punishment for sin, but from a perceptive recognition that these two great negatives interact, each increasing the power of the other. To avoid the pain of true aliveness I settle for 'partly living'. Not having fully lived, I cannot bear the thought of dying and reach for substitutes for aliveness. But they only increase my deadness, making me more unreal and callous, so that I feel not only half-alive but also guilty. I invest more effort in self-justification: I *must* feel alive while I have time and I *must* feel I am right, so – more substitutes and more desperation. St Paul calls this vicious circle 'the law, or principle, of sin and death'; it is the way things are, like the law of gravity. In his letter to the Christians at Rome he talks of death 'reigning', and of sin 'reigning' through death's agency (Rom. 8.2; 5.14, 17, 21). Never was this more monstrously demonstrated than in these days when the threat of a global death prompts no saner solution than the spending of ever more of the world's wealth on instruments of annihilation. Death rules, OK?

Now when I say that something is sin I am not necessarily pointing the finger of blame or trying to stir up feelings of guilt. I am simply stating that a particular action or attitude is harming a relationship with God, and that in order to put it right one must deal with God. I have called the deadness I see in so many lives and communities a malaise and a spiritual sickness. I am now saying that it injures people's relationship with the God who is more concerned that we be alive than that we be religious. And I am saying that those who want to come to life again must deal with God, whoever else they deal with. And this is good news. This is gospel. For God, the great giver, is also the great forgiver. 'God who is rich in mercy', says St Paul again, 'out of the great love with which he loved us even when we were dead in our falling away, brought us to life in union with Christ, and in union with him he raised us up' (Eph. 2.4–6).

How Jesus Christ comes into it – how he is instrumental in the forgiveness and in the bringing to life – is part of my theme in the next chapter. But at this point, in closing, I want to say how *you* come into it if you have identified yourself with anything I have said about the condition of deadness. The Christian word about the part human beings play in their own salvation is 'Repentance' – repentance supported by faith. Repentance doesn't mean sackcloth and ashes and the beating of breasts. It may mean tears, but they will be of joy and relief as much as of sorrow. Repentance means *turning* so as to face in another direction. In the matter we have been thinking about in this chapter, the matter of life and death, repentance will be an honest recognition of one's past choices of death rather than

life and a resolve to open oneself towards the renewal of awareness and response. You will need to pray for courage, for you
may remember how it hurts when the circulation returns to a
limb that has been numbed or frozen. But remember also that
he who has started to turn is already half-way home.

As an indication of what a repentance, a turning from one's
deadness towards the source of life might be, what words one
might use for such a prayer, I end by quoting from C. S. Lewis
in his autobiography *Surprised by Joy*:

The odd thing was that before God closed in on me, I was in
fact offered what now appears a moment of wholly free
choice. In a sense. I was going up Headington Hill on the
top of a bus. Without words and (I think) almost without
images, a fact about myself was somehow presented to me.
I became aware that I was holding something at bay, or
shutting something out. Of, if you like, that I was wearing
some stiff clothing, like corsets, or even a suit of armour, as
if I were a lobster. I felt myself being, there and then, given
a free choice. I could open the door or keep it shut; I could
unbuckle the armour or keep it on. Neither choice was
presented as a duty; no threat or promise was attached to
either, though I knew that to open the door or to take off
the corslet meant the incalculable. The choice appeared to
be momentous, but it was also strangely unemotional. I was
moved by no desires or fears. In a sense I was not moved by
anything. I chose to open, to unbuckle, to loosen the rein.[6]

O Living God,
we who are partly living,
scarely hoping,
and fitfully caring,
pray to you now
to make us fully alive.
Give us the vitality, awareness and commitment
that we see in Jesus Christ,
through the power of his death and resurrection.
We ask this in his Name.
Amen.

3

In Him Was Life

A few years ago *The Listener* carried the script of a radio talk by an American woman who has pioneered ameliorative work among the very old. She described a typical institution she had visited.

They were all sitting half dead in their wheel-chairs, mostly paralysed and just existing, they didn't live. They watched some television, but if you had asked them what they had watched they probably would not have been able to tell you. We brought in a young woman who was a dancer and we told her to play beautiful, old-fashioned music. She brought in Tchaikovsky records and so on and started to dance among these old people, all in their wheel-chairs, which had been set in a circle. In no time the old people started to move. One old man stared at his hand and said, 'Oh, my God, I haven't moved this hand in ten years.' And the 104-year-old, in a thick German accent, said 'That reminds me of when I danced for the Tsar of Russia.'[1]

I am struck by that story not merely as an account of a remarkable therapy, but as an instance of the effect of the really alive upon the half-dead or upon lifeless situations. And, in particular, it throws light on the impact of Jesus Christ upon his contemporaries.

But before I develop that theme I must take some account of the extreme scepticism with which many New Testament scholars regard all biographical statements about Jesus of Nazareth. They claim that the historical Jesus is simply not accessible to us for the following reasons.

1. The thought-world of first-century Palestine is so remote from ours that we can never be sure that their words convey to us the meaning they carried for them.

2. The material in the gospels emerged originally from oft-repeated sermons, liturgies and instructions in the faith and was brought together to reflect the individual insight of one or more authors; consequently we cannot say with certainty that any particular passage tells it as it actually occurred.

3. The gospels were written from the perspective of Christ's resurrection and lordship, so we can never get at the facts independently of that faith.

Now unless one believes, as many do, in a miraculous providence whereby the writings in the Bible were exempt from all the contingencies of normal communication, I think one has to acknowledge a degree of truth in those three caveats. But that means only that they constitute a challenge to further study, and to conclude that they make it historically impossible to know anything of the personality of Jesus strikes me as not only exaggerated but a strange abdication of the critical method itself.

A satisfactory examination of those three difficulties would require a complete course of study, and here I am only clearing the ground for something quite different. But for integrity's sake I must at least point towards a positive line of thought on each of the three, and I can quickly do so by reference to another great personality from the past who has shaped human thought and values, namely Socrates.

The thought-world of that fifth century BC and the context of his life and teaching is in many respects alien and actually inaccessible to our imaginations. Because we can be moved by the harmony of the bare bones of Greek temple ruins and the physical idealism of their sculptures, it does not mean that we have any conception of what such a temple communicated to its throng of worshippers as they processed from the bright sunshine into its dark interior dominated by the image of the god, heavy with the scents of flowers and incense and smoke and blood. Any classical dictionary can teach us the names of the gods and demigods of Greece and Asia Minor, but how can we with any empathy grasp what it was like to believe or disbelieve in the control of such beings? Who can tell with certainty what it was that Socrates experienced in the accompanying presence of that *daimonion*, or spirit, which was always with him? Yet, for all this incomprehension, it is no idle fiction to say we know the mind of Socrates and are challenged by it still. The bridge-building between cultures is perfectly possible.

The second difficulty raised by some scholars is the impossibility of knowing beyond dispute that this or that passage in the gospels is the authentic speech of Jesus, rather than a message which the second-generation church was anxious to convey. This also arises in the case of Socrates. He was a consummate teacher who left nothing in writing. What we know of him we owe to two of his greatest pupils, Plato the philosopher and Xenophon the historian. There is also a caricature of him in an early comedy by Aristophanes. Plato and Xenophon present somewhat different accounts of the contents of his teaching. There has been much argument as to which ideas should be attributed to him and which to his pupils. Yet there is no dispute about his character and personality or the effect he had upon people as one who combined great intellectual and moral genius. An inability to guarantee the separate details of a report does not in fact undermine the reliability of a historical portrayal nearly so much as has been made out.

And what of the lack of evidence concerning Jesus except from those who believed in his resurrection and saw all previous events in the light of it? It was just as impossible to assess the person and teaching of Socrates without seeing it illuminated by his martyrdom to truth. If he was in fact the kind of man who would eventually antagonize the guardians of convention and be condemned for irreligion and corrupting the minds of the young; if his nature was such that he must face death calmly and with humour; then that is how it can most truly be told. I am not suggesting that the resurrection and exaltation of Jesus were the natural *outcome* of the character of Jesus, though his death certainly was. But I am saying that even if there had been independent evidence, one would expect to find that his character had actually been consistent with a subsequent belief that God had uniquely raised him from the dead. In other words, hindsight is quite likely to produce the most truly historical story.

The original impulse of the whole Christian movement was the extraordinary conviction implanted against all common sense that Jesus was alive and present. He had been publicly executed by crucifixion and his corpse had been hastily buried. The whole thing had happened so suddenly that his followers were utterly unprepared and the blow must have shattered their hopes and their morale. We know that their state of mind was recalled afterwards as having been a kind of death. And then the next thing we know they are newborn into a living hope by a fact which they will be trying to pass on for the rest of their days: 'Jesus is alive and present.'

I shall be considering more thoroughly the meaning of that resurrection in the next chapter. The point I want to take up now is that no sooner did they begin to share this astounding announcement with others than they started to look back to the Jesus they had known before the catastrophe of his arrest and trial. There was no other way in which they could communicate their experience of his resurrection. It made no sense to talk about a risen Christ, a Lord and Saviour, unless they established a connection between their present experience and the man whom others could remember or had heard about. I cannot conceive how else the first groups of Christian believers in Jerusalem and elsewhere could proclaim a Christ of the church if they did not reiterate the broad outline of what was known of Jesus of Nazareth. This did not have to amount to an historian's interest; it was a simple necessity of communication. This is precisely what we see in the account of the earliest preaching in the Acts of the Apostles which, in the view of some New Testament scholars, does reflect the style of the first presentation of the gospel. 'Men of Israel, listen to me. I speak of Jesus of Nazareth, a man singled out by God . . . as you well know . . . You used heathen men to crucify and kill him . . . The Jesus we speak of has been raised by God, as we can all bear witness (Acts 2.22–4).

Of course, they were seeing with hindsight. They were looking back from beyond their experience of his resurrection.

And what they saw was continuity. They proclaimed, 'He is alive', and as they looked back they saw that 'alive' was what he had always been. It is the word that most adequately sums up the impact of Jesus upon his contemporaries. In the tradition of that earliest preaching of the apostles he is referred to as the 'Pioneer of life', or he 'who has led the way to life' (Acts 3.15) and the most theologically mature pronouncement about him in the New Testament is, 'In him was life' (John 1.4).

In chapter 1 I tried to show that aliveness in a human person has more to do with the quality of our consciousness than with mere physical vigour. To be really alive is to be alert and aware and responsive. Deadness, on the other hand, is lack of feeling, failure to notice, indifference. Damaged health may drag our spirits down, yet the aliveness I am speaking of burns often unabated in people who are victims of illness or adversity.

The figure of Jesus emerges in all the gospels as one who was supremely responsive and aware. The current of communication between himself and other individuals was never impaired, as it so often is with us. He could understand even the unspoken thoughts and respond to them. We read: 'He knew all people and had no need of evidence from others about anyone, for he knew what was in a person' (John 2.25). The critical host who was inwardly despising him over the dinner table found that out when Jesus suddenly brought the issue right into the open: 'Simon, I have something to say to you.' And he went on to tell a very pointed story (Luke 7.40–3). His powers of insight worked equally for those who needed encouragement. Who else in the over-crowded house could have guessed that what the sick man on the ground most wanted to hear were the words, 'Your sins are forgiven'? (Mark 6.5). There is no reason to read anything spooky into such incidents; it was the natural receptivity and sympathy of Jesus responding to the tiny signals and vibrations that all of us send out but so few people pick up. But in him, it seems, his sympathy reached such a degree of awareness that he was able to identify himself perfectly with another person. So it was that he noticed the unattractive little character perched in the tree above the heads of the crowd, and heard the cry of the blind beggar above the din (Luke 18.35–19.9). With the same quick awareness he looked at his future apostle, Simon Peter, and told him, 'You're Simon. One day you'll be called the Rock' (John 1.42). This immense aliveness to the truth of others was sometimes expressed humorously, as when he nicknamed others of his disciples besides 'the Rock.' There were the two brothers, Thunder's Boys, and that burly one known as 'Jude the Chest' (Thaddaeus).

Sensitivity, when it is wide awake, extends beyond one's fellow human beings to embrace all the small or humdrum things of daily life. Jesus had the natural poet's eye that saw significance in a cage of captive sparrows or a patch on an old coat. Neither the colours of the morning sky nor the beauty of a fading flower nor the dough in a kneading trough nor the cups and plates in the washing bowl, were beneath his notice. But it was a practical as well as a lyrical interest. He could attend to the left-overs after a picnic meal and make careful arrangements for a *rendez-vous* – a colt ready for the ride into Jerusalem, a secret guide to the house where they were to eat. Such mastery of detail was another aspect of the aliveness they remembered.

Above all, Jesus was portrayed as a man totally alive to God. As a Jewish boy he must have imbibed the idea of God from the observances of his family and the teaching of his synagogue

41

and local rabbi school. Yet he does not seem to have lived with a concept of God so much as a relationship to God. It was an affiliation of passionate intimacy and devotion. He clearly came to realize that other people did not apparently share or even desire such a relationship with God, and in one of his well-authenticated sayings he reached for a human analogy to explain it. 'No one knows a son like his own father, and no one knows a father so well as his son, and anyone to whom his son makes him known' (Matt. 11.27). That is how he felt his standing with God to be, and so he adopted the easy-going, child's word, 'Abba' for his prayers. The Fourth Gospel reports his saying, 'I know him, and if I said I did not, I should be a liar like you' (John 8.55). Hence the confident authority of his teaching: 'It was taught in the past, but now I say to you', as though his direct experience of God carried more weight than the precepts transmitted by tradition.[2] For him it was enough that people should model their treatment of others on God's treatment of us all. So, he said, Be loving to those who hate you for in that way you will be like your Father. You must have noticed that he sends rain on the sinners as well as the good ones, and his sun shines on just and unjust alike. Very disconcerting for the moralists! But 'set no limits to your goodness, as your heavenly Father is unlimited in his' (Matt. 5.44–8). The basis of your morality should be your knowledge of the nature of God so that you constantly say, If God is like *that*, how can we possibly go on treating people in this way?

That kind of simplicity generates an inner freedom, and freedom is another characteristic of the fully alive. All the four gospels offer the same overall impression of a human being who was breathtakingly free. It is, in fact, a disconcerting feature of his personality. In a society which valued reverence to parents very highly Jesus of Nazareth kept himself free from family ties. All the gospel traditions in their independence of each other contain some reflection of this distancing of Jesus from his mother.[3] Again, his attitude to property seemed to fit no known mould. He claimed to have no home to call his own and gave many warnings against wealth, yet could enjoy a party so obviously that his critics thought it reprehensible.[4] He said, 'If anyone wants to take your tunic let him have your cloak too', yet he seemed to consider it quite natural to knock up a neighbour for bread in the middle of the night, or to borrow someone else's boat or donkey when he needed it.[5] His motto seemed to be, 'Free to give, free to beg.' And his attitude to orthodoxy was no less disturbing. He observed the practices of his religion but refused to make it an absolute, because in his eyes everything was relative to something still to be revealed in the future. 'You worship something you do not know', he said to someone who was not an orthodox Jew. 'We know what we worship for salvation comes from our Jewish faith. But the time is coming, is coming now, when true worshippers will worship neither on your mountain here, nor in our Jerusalem, but will worship the Father in spirit and in truth' (John 4.22–3).

As he went forward he accepted the inevitable conflict between his vivid aliveness and the reaction of the frightened and conventional. That was only to be expected. Had not prophets always met with persecution? But it was painfully disappointing to find those who believed in him exhibiting the same deadness of spirit. When he spoke plainly of the conflict and its inevitable dénouement, they understood none of these things, what he said was obscure to them so that they could not grasp its meaning and they were afraid to ask him about it, and began to argue instead about which of them was the greatest. Unbelievable, isn't it? But the unaware are like that.

Yet these were the ones on whom he was going to have to rely. What was to be done to avert the failure of his mission? His aliveness must be transferred to them. His freedom must be theirs: 'I have come that they might have life and have it to the full.' 'If the Son sets you free, you will be truly free' (John 10.10; 8.36). The story I repeated at the beginning, about the girl whose dancing brought those half-dead elderly folk to life, is a parable of the transmission of life from Jesus Christ to those who came under his spell, and to all who do so still. The Fourth Gospel has him say, 'Because I am alive you shall come to life also' (John 14.19).

This is undoubtedly how we should understand his teaching of those crowds in Galilee. It was not just instruction. It was a transmission of life from the fully alive to the half dead. The mass of the people hung upon his words, and when he asked his chief apostle if he wanted to join those who were drifting away, the answer came back: 'To whom shall we go? Your words are words of eternal *life*' (John 6.68). And it is in connection with the hearing and heeding of his spoken word that the Fourth Gospel again has him say, 'The time is already here when the dead shall hear the voice of the Son of God and all who hear shall come to life' (John 5.24–6).

I believe that this perception of Jesus of Nazareth as a man so intensely alive that others catch life from his touch is the right way to understand those miracles of his. Healing of any kind is nine-tenths self-healing; the power of restoration is built into our very tissues, but so often it is suppressed by a countervailing burden of sheer exhaustion, physical damage or infection, fear, hopelessness or guilt. Someone, be it surgeon or physician, therapist or pastor, has to lift that burden enough to release the springs of health within the body and mind of the sufferer. In doing this it often happens that part of the burden is transferred to the helper. That is the process we see repeated in one story after another in the gospels as the aliveness of Jesus, his awareness and self-identification with others, is brought to bear upon overburdened men, women or children through a word or a touch. And in the exchange he was sometimes drained.[6]

The historical figure of Jesus that emerges almost incidentally from the study of the gospel material, then, is of a man supremely alive in his awareness and his freedom. He was, above everything else, alive, and his aliveness was contagious. The witness of the church, however, from its beginnings after the resurrection until now, has not been given in the past tense but the present: 'Jesus *is* alive and his aliveness is contagious.' Now that change of tense indicates far more than a sequel. Other characters in history have had something approaching the awareness and freedom of Jesus of Nazareth without thereby becoming candidates for resurrection. The return of his living human presence after his death lifted him out of a particular history into all history and made everything he had been and suffered universal. That self-identification of Jesus with others, which was an aspect of his aliveness, became all-inclusive at the end so that he took upon himself the whole human condition. And when his glorious awareness, sympathy and love engaged in its final encounter with the deadness, rigidity and fear of those who rejected him, the timeless issue between the power of life and the power of death was joined and fought out.

Life went down into death and was overwhelmed. The sensitive awareness of Jesus that had woken others to life made no impression on those who now ringed him round, neither on the set policies of the high priests nor the incomprehension of the Roman governor. Their inertness prevailed. In the long torture of his dying, darkness prevailed. With his last breath, death prevailed. It had to or it would not have been the death we suffer. There was nothing of him left – in the dramatist Tom Stoppard's words, 'only silence and some second-hand clothes'.[7] He who was Life itself had gone the whole way in identifying himself with our deadness.

This strange exchange which is effected when awareness becomes self-identification is the key to understanding Christianity. The fact that it is a normal, though peculiarly beautiful and mysterious human faculty does not disqualify it from being the means God has used to deal with us. It works as a kind of spiritual osmosis whereby pain or despair is drawn off from one to another, while endurance and hope flows from the other to the one. As an example, Mother Frances Dominica has allowed me to quote an experience which she described to me in these words.

I had known this mother for some time as both her daughters suffered from a rare genetic illness, and were frequent visitors to Helen House. During the year she and her husband went through a difficult and painful divorce. On Christmas morning she telephoned and I went. Her 13-year-old died the following morning, suddenly and unexpectedly. Seeing her sister dead, the four-year-old said, 'I wanted to die first', and five days later she too died. During those days and nights that I was with the mother and her children there were a thousand and one things to do. After the funeral there was nothing to do except to be there beside her.

Surrounded by grief too immense for words I felt physical pain which still recurs from time to time when I least expect it. By staying alongside I was absorbing a little of her pain.

On the cross the unparalleled aliveness of Jesus Christ went down under the deadness that is our sickness and our sin and was annihilated. Surrendering himself to death he drew it into himself and *absorbed* it. If you think of our deadness as sin, as we should, then you can see that it was absorbed in Christ's forgiveness; for that is how forgiveness works – it absorbs the wrong by enduring the pain and hostility of it without throwing it back. And if you think of our deadness as a wasting disease you can see that its infection spent itself upon Christ, and was absorbed or, as the New Testament puts it, 'swallowed up'.

Bring together those two stories – of Mother Frances taking upon herself the pain for which there were no words, and of that young dancer making over her animation to the half-dead – and you can grasp the meaning of the Christian eucharist. In that simple ritual Jesus Christ bequeathed to his followers down the centuries a very direct, very basic means by which his own perfect aliveness might be imparted to them; and, through the same action, an enduring token of the eternal cost of that sharing. The bread is broken as he was, the wine poured into the cup as his life was poured out. Then it is offered – offered to his Father as his whole being was, in all its awareness and responsiveness, and then offered to us. 'Because I am alive you shall be alive also.' It isn't forced upon anyone, nor does anyone receive it simply by sitting back and doing nothing. That would only confirm us in our deadness and non-response. So he says, *Take* it. He says, *Ask*. He says, *Come*. How you do that or what you say is between you and him. His real aliveness is on offer. Choose life!

Lord Jesus Christ,
alive and at large in the world,
help me to follow and find you there today,
in the places where I work,
meet people,
spend money,
and make plans.
Take me as a disciple of your kingdom,
to see through your eyes,
and hear the questions you are asking,
to welcome all others with your trust and truth,
and to change the things that contradict God's love,
by the power of the cross
and the freedom of your Spirit.
Amen.

4

Resurrection

I said in the last chapter that the initial impetus of the whole Christian movement and its enduring message for the world is contained in the words: Jesus is alive! That is what they meant, and they were saying it about the Jesus they had known and who had died. What they actually said was 'Jesus is Lord!' and 'The Lord is risen!' The implications of that exultant shout are staggering, and in pursuing the theme of Life and Death I have tried to show how far those implications reach into every sector of our human condition. In this chapter we shall home in to this central conviction and think about the resurrection faith.

Faith in the resurrection of Jesus has sometimes been misunderstood by Christians themselves and misrepresented in their preaching and their religious art. Consequently it has been made even harder for everyone to understand and to believe than need have been the case, though nothing can take away the inherent difficulty. So from the start the Christians' extraordinary claim has been explained away by one method or another, and the controversy is active still.

I am anxious not to shift into an argumentative key for very long because my purpose is different; but I must set out quite simply my reasons for continuing to believe in the resurrection of Jesus as the church has taught it.

I believe in the resurrection of Jesus because leaderless and hopeless groups of people do not quite suddenly become irrepressibly confident unless something has happened to cause the change; and that sudden change certainly did take place. Again, the extraordinary message they began to proclaim was that *God* had raised Jesus up from death; they considered it was an act of God. But people only talk about 'acts of God' when there has been some physical event for them to explain in that way. Something must have happened 'within history' to call for an interpretation that lies beyond history.

I believe in the resurrection of Jesus because of the ring of truth that pervades the gospels which include the accounts of it. I realize this is a subjective and literary judgment. Yet I am certain that if the first generation of Christians had been like any other cult inspired by delusions concerning its founder, its resurrection-stories would have been far more weird and fevered; and if those stories had been fabrications piously devised to augment faith, such deliberate embroiderers could never have created the integrity or the moral stature of the figure of Jesus in the gospels. The style would have been different, as it is, in fact, in so-called 'gospels' that were written later.

But I also believe in the resurrection of Jesus because I am one of the millions whose experience of a relationship with God, which is also a relationship with him, compels them to say even today, 'Jesus is alive', meaning by that something much more actual than if I were to say 'Mozart is alive'. This is unsatisfactory as evidence, but, none the less, belief in

Christ's resurrection is inseparable from that unique and undeniable relationship.

In passing on their faith in Christ's resurrection those first Christians naturally repeated and preserved different stories, and each of the gospels has woven a few of these into its account. The stories are of two kinds: some are about the tomb of Jesus being found open and empty, and some are about his appearing to various people. Many think that the stories about the empty tomb began to be told a good deal later than the others, but the only evidence for this is that St Paul never referred to them in his letters which, of course, were written before the Gospels. He does, however, make quite a lot of the burial of Christ as the prelude to his resurrection. So, while he may not have known about the finding of the empty tomb, all one can say with certainty is that it had not been passed on to him as fundamental to faith in Christ's resurrection, and certainly not as the proof of it. But the suggestion that the stories about the tomb were made up at a later date to strengthen belief in the reality of the resurrection does not stand up well in the face of two features in these accounts. Would anyone inventing a story to confirm the belief have made *women* the witnesses of the empty tomb, seeing that the evidence of women was disallowed in those days as a matter of proof? St Luke's Gospel, in fact, actually draws attention to this difficulty. Then again, why should someone telling the story for effect have introduced a detail of the Jewish arrangement of grave cloths which has confused the church outside Palestine ever since? It reads more like someone simply telling it as it was.

The other type of story tells how Jesus 'appeared' to people on various occasions. This was the tradition handed on to St

Paul about three years after the crucifixion of Jesus, and he regarded his own encounter on the Damascus road as another such 'appearance' of the risen Christ. The word 'he appeared' means more than 'he was seen', as though it might have been a subjective vision. The form of the verb implies that Jesus was the real subject: 'He showed himself', or even, perhaps, that it was God's action: 'He was revealed.'[1] What they encountered was Jesus in an entirely new kind of existence, Jesus raised up, exalted. It was none the less a real encounter with Jesus himself in his total humanity, not as ghost nor as pure spirit isolated from the body. That Greek idea of separate components of the human person was foreign to the thought of the Bible. So it seems that this new mode-of-being embraced in some way the body that had died on the cross.

But we trivialize the resurrection if we think of the risen Christ simply as someone brought back to life. Though he shows himself and is recognized in an amazing normality, he belongs more to the invisible than the visible world, and his departures do not withdraw his presence. He is no longer confined to their framework of space and time. He is the same Jesus but now universal and at large in all the world. His nearness to them is something they experience similarly to God's nearness. Yet even that is a kind of expansion of how things were before, when his words and his companionship had brought God closer. Perhaps the best indication of what his risen presence began to mean is caught in the words in St John's Gospel: 'I will not leave you bereft; I am coming back to you. In a little while the world will see me no longer. But you will see me. Because I live you too will come alive. Then you will know that I am in my Father and you in me and I in you. Whoever receives my commands and obeys them, that is the one who loves me. And whoever loves me will be loved by my Father. And I will love and reveal myself to that one' (14.18–21).

To take in what this revelation of Jesus, living and exalted, must have meant to them, and could mean to us, we should use our imaginations. They were a cluster of broken men and women. But they had formerly been living in a confused elation of spiritual renewal and political expectancy, carried along by the vitality of a leader whose presence brought God so near, and made his will so clear, that it was like living in heaven already. He had trusted his God like a child. He had got them trusting God in the same way and actually modelling their behaviour on what they knew this God was like. And now just when it seemed that a new day was about to dawn for all the desperate and downtrodden people of the land, God had let their leader down. Not only had his enemies suddenly pounced but the Father God he had trusted hadn't raised a finger to help him, and he had died after a cry of absolute forsakenness. Far worse than his betrayal by Judas was his betrayal by God. So there was nothing left for them to believe in. The rest of life was meaningless and absurd.

And there was the added pain of their own unforgivable betrayal. They too had let him down. Pretending they didn't know him, had nothing to do with him, they had left him to face it all alone. He might have forgiven them even this, for he was incredible about forgiving people. But he wasn't there any more; and they couldn't forgive themselves.

Yet suddenly they are tumbling out into the streets of Jerusalem, talking in clear unrestrained voices, and one phrase thrown back and forth like a refrain, 'The Lord is risen' – 'Risen indeed'. Naturally you would say, 'What on earth has happened now?' And you would be right to jump to the conclusion that *something* had happened, something beyond themselves and their mental state. If you had had any idea of the condition these women and men had been in, you would dismiss me as a fool if I answered: 'They have just realized that Jesus' body lies a-mouldering in the grave but his soul goes marching on. Or perhaps they have had a corporate hallucination and imagine they have seen Jesus standing among them.' No, something must have happened, and the simple gist of it was that Jesus was living and present, and his aliveness and nearness brought them to life again and brought God near once more. Wasn't this just how he had affected them in Galilee in the days before the tragedy? But now it was happening at an altogether different level. 'Because I am alive,' he had said, 'you shall be alive too.' This was news they had to share more widely. 'Praise be to the God and Father of our Lord Jesus Christ who in his great mercy gave us new birth into a living hope by the resurrection of Jesus Christ from the dead' (I Peter 1.3).

There was a link between this man and God closer than anything they had imagined possible. They had certainly begun to sense this during his brief public life; now the link was immeasurably more clear. They would never be able to think of God except as *his* God, *his* Father. They would know God through him. In the words of Archbishop Ramsey, God was now forever Christ-like.[2] In a way that they could not immediately grasp and which would take a lot of thinking out, the appalling let-down of his crucifixion was not so senseless and devoid of God as they had supposed. It was 'for us'. It was 'for our sins'.

But neither could they again think of him apart from God.

They would always know him now *in* God. Their continuing relationship with him would be essentially a relationship with God. Words written much later might have described what they even then felt to be their relationship – their life was 'hidden with Christ in God' (Col. 3.3).

Now something stranger followed. I quote from Lucas Grollenberg's book, *Jesus*.

> They had become new men with new hopes and new expectations. Moreover what had happened to them seemed to be catching. They felt that they had to pass their experiences on to others, and when those others heard the story, they too were captivated by it. They too found a new way of looking at themselves and the world around, and they too were seized with a new hope.[3]

In a word, the story of Jesus, especially of his death and resurrection, told years afterwards to those who never met him, affected them in exactly the same way as the resurrection had affected the broken and hopeless companions of Jesus at the beginning. The resurrection of Jesus was, and is, still going on, both as a personal encounter with Jesus as the Lord, the Living One, and as a coming-to-life on the part of the hearers. The one follows from the other, so that St Paul can speak about people being 'brought to life with Christ, even when we were dead in our sins' and of being 'raised up together with Christ Jesus' (Eph. 2.5, 6).

A kid from the New York slums can say: 'I know this is real. And you know how? Because Jesus Christ seemed to come right out of the Bible. He became a living person who wanted to stand with me through my problems.'[4] Don't too hastily dismiss such talk as childish or emotional. The sophisticated cosmopolitan, Thomas Merton, recalling his deepening but still uncommitted interest in the early churches of Rome, wrote:

> The saints of those forgotten days had left upon the walls of their churches a word which I was able in some measure to apprehend. But above all the most real and most immediate source of my new knowledge was Christ himself, present in those churches, and it was he who was teaching me who he was more directly than I was capable of realizing.[5]

But these personal 'Easters', like the resurrection of Jesus himself, must involve our total integrated being and may never be confined to our spirits in isolation. If we come to life at all we come to life in our complete humanity, and other people are going to notice a difference. Indeed, they may not merely observe a new aliveness in us but we and they together may be caught in a corporate coming to life of a whole community. That is what seems to have followed from the resurrection of Jesus. It was not a transformation in Simon Peter alone with which the others went along, but the rebirth of a whole body of men and women within a very short time. After all, the event which most resembles a resurrection in the pages of the Old Testament, and out of which the language of resurrection first became current, was a national re-creation, the return of the Jewish people from their exile in Babylonia. This was the burden of Ezekiel's prophecies: 'Man, these bones are the whole people of Israel. They say, "Our bones are dry, our thread of life is snapped, our web is severed from the loom." Prophesy, therefore, and say to them, "These are the words of the Lord God: O my people, I will open your graves and bring you up from them and restore you to the land of Israel. You shall know that I am the Lord when I open your graves and bring you up from them, O my people. Then I will put my spirit into you and you shall live, and I will settle you on your own soil, and you shall know that I the Lord have spoken and will act" ' (Ezek. 37.11–14). In that passage, and in the preceding chapter of Ezekiel, moral cleansing, spiritual renewal, political liberation and economic security are given equal weight as elements in the full salvation of Israel which is going to bring honour to the name of their Saviour-God.

History is full of such communal resurrections and we do well to remember them lest we narrow the Christian hope to purely individual salvations and cut ourselves off from those whose prayer and struggle is for a liberation of their whole community. Again and again that hope may be disappointed, or else realized only on a lamentably small scale, yet its renewal in the hearts of the apparently defeated is one of the most miraculous aspects of our coming to life. The ghastly magnitude of the 'holocaust', for example, has blinded most people to the real 'resurrection' of those who survived and whose liberation was so like that of the exiled Jews from Babylon. One of them has told how he and his fellow-prisoners reacted during the days when they were freed but not yet able to travel elsewhere. On the first day they walked in the countryside around the camp, but were incapable of feeling any joy. They returned, bewildered and apathetic, to eat ravenously. He goes on:

One day, a few days after the liberation, I walked through the country past flowering meadows, for miles and miles, toward the market town near the camp . . . There was no one to be seen for miles around; there was nothing but the wide earth and sky and the larks' jubilation and the freedom of space. I stopped, looked around, and up to the sky – and then I went down on my knees . . . I know that on that day, in that hour, my new life started. Step for step I progressed, until I again became a human being.[6]

Whether we experience resurrection as individuals or in some corporate break-through, it is going to be real and specific and won't be limited to the invisible realm of our souls. If we are grasped by the aliveness and the lordship of Jesus Christ our own waking-up may actually start in some quite secular change of direction. I have already made the point and I must stress it again. By raising and exalting Jesus, God gave him all authority in heaven and on earth, authority over earthly as well as heavenly realities. A lot of Christians and other religious folk would like religion to be full of heavenly questions: Is there a God? What must I do to win eternal life? When a sincere young man put that second question to Jesus he got an answer he had not bargained for. Out of great love for him and because he took him seriously, Jesus 'earthed' his reply: 'Sell up your properties and give everything to the poor.' In our appeal to people we shrink from making faith so specific. But Jesus could see that, for that particular man, his investments were the place where he had to make a break for life. That was where the new birth must take place or not at all.

For different people the coming to life needs to start, if it is ever going to, at some other point of decision – such as when a well-established, inwardly insecure father made the first sympathetic move towards a better understanding with his eldest daughter, idealistically contemptuous of her parents' way of life; or when a city councillor screwed up her courage to withstand her party colleagues over a policy she had long felt to be unjust; or when a young couple, both temperamentally negative and depressed, agreed not to have an abortion in spite of a certain degree of risk. These examples illustrate my point, not because the decision was intrinsically right, but because in each case it was a vote for life. And for them the reality of Jesus Christ constituted an invitation to come alive in that way and also offered a source of faith and courage.

But the resurrection of Jesus does more than inspire us to take the particular step that may lead to fullness of life. His cross and resurrection reveal the secret of all aliveness, his and ours. Life is renewed through the habitual laying down of life. 'In truth, in very truth', says Jesus Christ, 'I tell you a grain of wheat remains a solitary grain, unless it falls into the ground and dies; but if it dies it bears a rich harvest' (John 12.24). 'Whoever wishes to hold on to life is lost. But if any will let themselves be lost, for my sake and the gospel's, that one is safe. What does a person gain by winning the whole world at the cost of the true self?' (Mark 8.35–6). Death followed by resurrection, life through dying, this is the way things are. It is not a truth limited to the one event of Christ's death and resurrection, nor does it affect us only when we approach the end of our lives. It is a principle of all existence. The pattern of real aliveness is set before us in the dying and rising of Jesus. We can see it vividly in the movement of Ria Bancroft's beautiful bronze relief that is reproduced on the cover of this book: down into the loss and finality of death, then up into the surge of new life.

But that is also the basic movement of a baptism. Down into the waters of death – such an ancient and universal symbol –

but then, through that death, out and up into newness of life. Christian baptism was never meant to convey less than that. It unites us with the Christ who died for us and lives. It unites us with his dying and with his resurrection life. And, in that bond with him, it commits us to the pattern of all true liveliness, the pattern of life through death, as the way for our own responding and deciding.

'Have you forgotten,' St Paul wrote to the Romans, 'that when we were baptized into union with Christ Jesus we were baptized into his death? By baptism we were buried with him and lay dead, in order that, as Christ was raised from the dead in the splendour of the Father, so also we might set our feet upon the new path of life. For if we have become incorporate with him in a death like his, we shall also be one with him in a resurrection like his' (Rom. 6.3–5).

Life through death. It is the pattern of every human birth. To the baby it must certainly feel like dying, and a violent death at that. The only existence it has known, a marvellously secure and balanced form of life, has broken down, and the last moorings with reality are cast off – which is just what happens at the end of our earthly story too. The desperate infant cannot know that an infinitely more free and richer life awaits it when that dying has been done. It has never realized that already, in the old life which it is losing, it has been forming an equipment for the new life beyond – lungs and eyes and voice – which remain dormant and meaningless until that future existence has begun.

If that is the experience of being born, it is equally the experience of being born again – the fullness of life that is the theme of this book. The dying is what the New Testament calls repentance – recognizing the seriousness and the sin of my own deadness, my refusals of life, my running away from real life. Turning towards Christ, the giver and forgiver. Letting go, and letting God. Then, after that death of repentance, there is the lifting up into a new kind of aliveness and freedom.

But it doesn't end there. In any lifetime, Christian or not, there are innumerable little deaths – always painful and frightening (that can't be avoided): the failure of an exam and change of course, perhaps; the break-up of a love affair; the loss of a childish faith; seeing one's child leave home for the first time; moving house; the loss of a job; retirement. Cling to what you have at that moment, and you're lost. Unclench your hands and let it slip away, and you are ready to receive the unimagined new life. If we can learn that habit from all the small occasions for dying which may come to us, then when the last letting-go is called for, it will be familiar and confident. Our formation of that habit will be immeasurably strengthened as we keep our eyes on the truth about God and about life revealed in Jesus, whose attitude was: 'I lay down my life to receive it back again. No one has robbed me of it. I am laying it down of my own free will. I have the inner authority to lay it down and to receive it back again. This charge I received from my Father' (John 10.17–18).

This is the true cost of living. Always a death – for the father making his vulnerable first move to restore a relationship with his daughter; for the woman councillor courting the loss of her party's support; for the couple risking death in order to vote for life.

In the ninth year of our service in Uganda an unexpected change in our family situation made it necessary for us all to return to this country. This was a reversal of all we had planned and hoped. Of course it had real compensations, yet it was a very painful wrench and the disappointment grew worse when, after a year, I still had no other job. I felt absurdly angry with God, and took it out on my innocent family in a nasty, prolonged grouchiness. Slowly and painfully I was brought to see that what I resented losing was a childishly romantic image of myself as a lifelong Christian missionary. It was my spiritual self-importance that had to die. Then the way opened for me to return to Africa for short periods of research in a very down-to-earth role. I was brought into a more complete and intimate experience of Africa than ever I met when wearing a missionary hat. I don't for a moment disparage the superb contributions of other missionaries; I know only that for me the new style of contact brought an opening of my eyes that enriched my whole understanding of life and of Christianity.

It is an even more convincing experience of resurrection when a community or an institution dies in order to go forward to a fuller life, and one that we should believe in and pursue more boldly. Rarely have I seen a building of more monumental irrelevance to its environment than the Anglican cathedral in Calcutta once was. It enshrined the patrician ideals of the best of the British imperial rulers and its shining Gothic splendour nodded acquaintance with the classical palaces of the great trading companies and banks across the Maidan. But what on earth had it to do with the swarming humanity of Calcutta or the poverty-stricken Church of North India? Following the transfer of leadership in church and state, the cathedral seemed to be wrapped in a dream of the past.

Then came the war in Bangladesh. Exhausted and bewildered refugees poured over the frontiers and the Indian government did its best to provide them with minimal services. The cathedral office under its Indian dean had already become the centre for a consortium of Christian service organizations in the city, and now they took up the challenge of the refugees as well. The barn-like cathedral became a barn in fact, the main clearing house for material aid. The spacious driveway, designed for vice-regal carriages, was churned by heavy trucks and the marble steps were chipped by the edges of crates and canisters. The congregation, which grew beyond all previous records, moved forward along narrow alleys between towering walls of rice sacks, flour bags and blankets, to receive communion with a deeper sense of the Mystery than ever. The great Victorian galleries became the workrooms in which hundreds of yards of tarpaulin were stitched into tents and bivouacs. It was a disfigured death of many cherished values, but what a coming to life was there!

So the choice for every human being is between death or death – the death of a letting-go that hurts like hell but leads to resurrection, or the death of slow extinction as all the energies are spent on getting and keeping, instead of living and giving.

Father,
if the hour has come
to make the break,
help me not to cling,
even though it feels like death.
Give me the inward strength
of my Redeemer, Jesus Christ,
to lay down this bit of life
and let it go,
so that I and others may be free
to take up whatever new and fuller life
you have prepared for us,
now and hereafter.
Amen.

5

The Living God

At the end of the third chapter I brought together two incidents: the story of the young girl whose dancing for the half-dead old people handed on some of her vivacity to them and brought them to life, and Mother Frances Dominica's experience of physically absorbing into her own body some of the suffering of that bereaved mother. You will remember that I tried to draw from both these stories an understanding of what Jesus Christ was doing for humanity in his death and resurrection, and of what we believe he is offering to us in the sacrament of the Bread and Wine.

This strange and beautiful faculty of exchanging something of one another's inmost self is an extension of that mutual awareness which I said in chapter 1 is the essence of being really alive. It is the highest expression of the mode of relationship that Martin Buber described as a mutual giving: 'You say *Thou* to it and give yourself to it, it says *Thou* to you and gives itself to you.' To be really alive to another person is to make oneself open to that sort of exchange.

I have borrowed that word 'exchange' from a book by Rosemary Haughton called *The Passionate God*. In it she sets out to show that some kind of interchange and commutation is the activating principle of all existence as we know it. So she reminds us of the original fiery state of this globe in which chemicals were formed and re-formed through an escalating complexity of giving out and receiving back; of the erosion of the oldest rocks, the surrender of their particles to the oceans and their reconstitution there as the younger rocks; of the ceaseless interflow of energies in the cells of organisms and the interdependence of living creatures.[1]

At a lowly level, then, a kind of 'exchange' seems to be a condition of existence. To *be* anything is to act upon and be acted upon. The moon is a dead world where not much goes on, yet it moves our seas and is held by our gravitational field. But how much more interaction there is in the phenomena of our *living* world! Impact and response, giving and receiving, are the very essence of life, and the more intensely life is lived the more delicate and penetrating the 'exchange' becomes. What in my first chapter I called awareness, or the opening of the eyes, is actually a mutual communication, an interflow, and this is what we should always mean by the word 'life'.

Now, remembering that, we can better grasp the sheer strength and surprise of that revelation which dominates the Old Testament that God is 'the *living* God'. The word is always used to contrast the Hebrew people's understanding of God with that of others. It is an exile among the temples of Assyria or Babylon who sings in Psalm 42, 'My soul thirsteth for God, for the *living* God.' The boy David goes forth to challenge the huge champion of the polytheist invaders with the words, 'Who is this uncircumcised Philistine that he should defy the armies of the *living* God?' (I Sam. 17.26). Here is a typical passage from a prayer by one of the prophets making this derisive comparison:

> Where among the wisest of the nations and all their royalty can one be found like thee? They are fools and blockheads one and all, learning their nonsense from a log of wood. The beaten silver is brought from Tarshish and the gold from Ophir; all are the work of craftsmen and goldsmiths. They are draped in violet and purple, all the work of skilled men. But the Lord is God in truth, a *living* God (Jer. 10. 7–10).

We may find that scornful and triumphalist dismissal of the sacred images of other religions distasteful today; but the point I want to get at is why the contrast is summed up in the word 'living'. It is precisely because they understood that God partakes of that 'exchange', that awareness and response, acting upon and being acted upon, which we have just called the essence of life. It is the non-reaction, the deadness, not just of the images but of the conception of God they represent that disqualifies them in the eyes of the prophets and psalmists. By the same token, no doubt, the Hebrews would have found inadequate the immovable and unaffected deity of the philosophers. 'They have mouths that cannot speak, and eyes that cannot see; they have ears that cannot hear, nostrils, and cannot smell; with their hands they cannot feel, with their feet they cannot walk, and no sound comes from their throats. Their makers grow to be like them, and so do all who trust in them' (Ps. 115.5–8).

We don't, of course, take literally all those phrases in the Bible that attribute human actions and emotions to God, neither did the writers themselves. But when they speak so boldly of a God who rises up early, who raises the battle cry, who regrets his own actions, who laughs, is jealous, gasps like a woman in labour, or yearns with love, they are simply insisting that God is a reactive God who gives himself in the exchange, the interflow which is life.

Now we may readily accept the truth of this as an account of God's relationship with human beings or even with the whole creation. He is, as Psalm 36 puts it, 'the fountain of life'. All flows from him. 'All that has come into existence is alive with his life' (John 1.3, 4). We may even allow that there is a mutuality, a flow-back, in his relation to the creation that can truly be expressed in those startlingly human phrases in the Bible. But what of God in himself, in his eternal transcendence?

To think of God in himself is, strictly, beyond the power of human thought. He is not a being that speculation might conceive. He is not even the supreme being. He is 'Being' itself. Yet we are given clues and they confirm the truth that God in himself, Being itself, consists of what we have called 'exchange'. The name I AM, which the Jews regarded as so directly expressing God's being that they would never pronounce it, carries in Hebrew a dynamic sense: not merely 'I am' in a static state of being, but 'I am present', or 'I am for', as though even that ultimate Awareness consisted of interflow.

Now this was not the line of argument that led the early church eventually to formulate its doctrine of the Trinity. Yet that Christian understanding of the nature of God in himself does aptly endorse the idea that 'exchange' lies at the very heart of the being of God, the living God. One can say this without suggesting that there are three distinct centres of knowing, 'three gods', in the One Deity; for even in the inadequate analogy of our individual self-consciousness we can discern a dynamic dialogue between our sense perceptions, our thoughts about them and our evaluation of them, so that it is precisely when we are aware of holding a conversation within ourselves that we are most whole and most alive. This precious insight of Christian thought affirms that Being itself is an eternal giving and receiving. The same is said more simply in the words, 'God is love' – not 'God is a loving God,' nor 'God is ever ready to love,' but 'God *in himself* is love.'

Something of this truth is discovered by those who persevere in their prayers beyond the level of asking for things to the point where prayer is communion with God or simply being in his presence. They tell of becoming aware of being 'prayed through', as though they themselves were only the instrument, the telephone wire, for the flow of communication of God with God, the interchange of the eternal love and joy. This is surely what St Paul was describing when he wrote about the Holy Spirit standing in for us to augment our weak ignorant prayer (Rom. 8.26–27). This experience of those who have gone some way into prayer 'fits' remarkably with those more momentary but unforgettable encounters with the reality of God which so many people have occasionally experienced even when they were wholly out of touch with any religious practice or belief. I referred to a few such accounts in my opening chapter. Transient and highly individual these intimations of God's presence certainly are, yet they convey to the one who receives them a sense of being caught up into an immense pervading joy of giving and receiving that embraces and unifies all things.

Life, of which this dynamic, living God is the source, is relationship. The deadness, which is our sin against life, comes from our refusal of exchange, our shutting off of self so as neither to give nor receive. Being brought to life is the renewal of relationship with this living God and, in him, with all creatures.

It follows, then, that the life of the fully alive cannot be sustained in isolation or privacy, but must express itself in community. This does not mean clubs and cliques or general *bonhomie*. It means being open, whenever the opportunity is afforded, for those exchanges whereby the aliveness and freedom of the one flows to the other, or the pain and darkness of the other is shared and taken upon the one.

That was the kind of interrelationship that was held up as the ideal for the ancient Hebrews as the people of that living God. They never completely fulfilled the ideal pattern, and even the regulations in which the ideal was presented reflected the incomplete perceptions of those times, as any attempt to set down God's way for a human community is bound to do. Nevertheless we can see in the details of their social laws the dream of 'Shalom', a community that was meant to reflect the exchange of care and respect between all creatures. The poor, the unfortunates, the aliens were to be remembered and room made for them in the scheme of things. When they reaped their harvests they were not to retrace their steps to gather what had been dropped or left uncut in the corners of the cornfields. Others would be glad of that. When vines or olive trees were picked they were not to be gone over a second time. If anyone came on a wild fowl sitting on eggs they must not take both bird and eggs for their larder. It was a principle of live and let live, of fitting oneself into the pattern of the whole; it pursued the ideals of ecology before that word was invented. And this was to be the way of it because that is what it means to be alive. These were the people who had said they had chosen life rather than death. They were the people who worshipped the living God. Then let them be alive, alive to the reality of others and of all creatures, aware of the whole for which they were to be answerable to that God.

The same pattern of mutality and exchange was set before the communities of the first Christians as the *milieu* in which alone their aliveness in Christ was to be lived out. They were in no position then to change the great structures of the Roman empire or model society on their new-found vision of aliveness to one another in Christ. Most of them came from the polyglot slave population. Yet within their own gatherings they were called to come alive to one another's reality in a new way. Instead of the universal covetousness, the 'more-and-more' sickness, they were to cultivate the strange new virtue called *epieikēs*, 'fitting in'. 'Let your fitting into the whole be patent to everyone,' wrote St Paul to the Philippians.[2] Their awareness of one another in Christ must mean that for them there were no more distinctions and separations of Jews and Gentiles, or of slaves and free, or of men and women. Rich and poor were to become mutually aware and caring in a new way. There were to be no double standards on that score any more. But beyond these specific changes of attitude, they were called to a mutuality in depth – confiding in one another, forgiving one another, hearing one another's burdens, building one another up. That word rings like a theme song through the pages of the New Testament. It is the word which sums up the exchange of self with self which burns in the being of the living God and should burn in the reflected aliveness of God's people.

But it never has, neither in the Jewish community in the days of the Old Testament and since, nor in the Christian church as a whole. Here and there it has really happened, the aliveness and interchange of the people of God reflecting the exchange in the being of that living God. It has happened often enough for us still to imagine what it might be, so that hope has never died. It has been seen under the pressure of great persecution when loyalty and faith became basic. It can be seen in places where the church is exhilaratingly new and simple, or at times of spiritual renewal (when 'renewal' itself has not been turned into a stereotype and a jargon). It can be seen when Christians are united in their resistance to some grave injustice or entrenched evil and there is no room left for pettiness or compromise. But for most of the time the church, whichever branch you look at, is humiliatingly disappointing and a major obstacle to belief in God. In saying that one needs to be fair and not criticize the church's institutionalism. You cannot preserve a tradition or pass a gospel on from generation to generation without a framework of authorities and regulations and organization. This is true of a university or an orchestra, a nation or a church. They are all systems, and systems are essential. But systems, structures and institutions, just like individuals, have to choose between life and death, over and over again. The church, or any Christian group or society, is prone to grow the hard crust of self-protection, prone to run away from life, prone to find substitutes for being fully alive. This is why I have chosen the theme of life and death, so that it is equally pertinent to us all, whether we call ourselves Christians or not. What does our baptism avail us if, as a church, we are refusing to let some cherished thing die in order that we may be brought more fully to life?

So when anyone comes to life in the ways I have tried to describe, through the awareness which is the Holy Spirit's gift or through an awakening to the living reality of Christ, joining a church or Christian group may not seem the most obvious next step or, if it does, the Christian fellowship on first acquaintance may make the same impression as that well-mannered family which fails to make one feel at home or fully oneself.

Yet the church, as it is, is all we have got and we cannot do without it. Neither you nor I can be Christian in isolation, since the aliveness we receive from Christ and the Spirit of God consists of exchange and 'one-anotherness'. Willy-nilly any church you might like to invent, or any body of people with whom you might choose to live out your new-found aliveness, is going to exist in a perpetual choice of life or death, since that is true of every one of us. At any moment and in any circumstances the Christians who are there are capable of becoming more alive, and sometimes a simple thing starts the transformation.

So how should someone with a newly-found faith, or some Christian of long standing who has newly come alive, identify herself or himself with a Christian congregation in a way that will confirm and increase the new life more than it disenchants and deadens? To such a one I would say, 'Come as a learner; come as a dreamer; come as a pioneer.'

Come as a learner, even if you are one who has heard it all before. With the gift of new awareness you should see old truth in a fresh light and find yourself expressing it in unfamiliar terms. And that may be disconcerting for you and for others. Don't be too readily domesticated and house-trained, but come, all the same, as a learner. You have become a citizen of an unfamiliar kingdom. You have a language to learn and a history to make your own and customs to adopt in order to share in its heritage. And, as often happens, the natives may be more ignorant of their own culture than they think, and your enquiries may start them learning too. That also is an example of 'exchange'! But in all your learning remember that the scriptures you are trying to understand and beginning to love, the words and the shape of the worship that is becoming more familiar, the unknown territory of personal prayer you are starting to explore, the books and discussions and activities that are yours within the Christian fellowship, all have one purpose only: to make the vision of Christ clearer to you and all the church and, through an enlivened church, to everyone.

But come also as a dreamer. In the mutual awareness and exchange of a living fellowship the church should trade its tradition for your dreams. That is how, in the words of Jesus, it can always bring out of its treasury things new and old (Matt. 13.52). If you retain your inner aliveness by the grace of God, you will feel the pain of a church that has, perhaps, settled for partly living. It will be moderately eager to pass on its tradition to a learner, but not particularly interested in dreams of what it might have been. Don't be silenced, for the freshness of your idealism, whatever your age may be, renews the youth of the whole church. The vision of freedom, aliveness and exchange, of the divine life reflected in human community, has been finely portrayed in a poem by A. S. J. Tessimond.

> One day people will touch and talk, perhaps, easily,
> And loving be natural as breathing and warm as
>   sunlight;
> And people will untie themselves as string is unknotted,
> Unfold and yawn and stretch and spread their fingers,
> Unfurl, uncurl, as seaweed returned to the sea.

And work will be simple and swift as a seagull flying,
And play will be casual and quiet as a seagull settling;
And the clocks will stop, and no one will wonder or
care or notice,
And people will smile without reason, even in winter,
even in the rain.[3]

There will be those who are quick to point out, not only
that such poetic wishful-thinking is too flimsy to support faith
or give practical guidance, but that it expresses a humanistic
hope for society as a whole rather than God's promises to his
own people. I could have chosen other poems from the Bible
itself – visions of a day when every man should sit unafraid
beneath his own vine and his own fig tree; visions of swords
being beaten into ploughshares; visions of a city full of boys
and girls playing in its streets. They are all unashamedly dreams
of the human community as a whole. They are Everyman's
dreams. What makes the church distinctive is not that its
hopes are for its own future alone, but that it knows who the
Desire of all Nations is. Christians must always embrace the
world, its hungers and its hopes, in their strategy. The church
can be the faithful church only when its concern is for the human
community as a whole. St Paul served a vision that encom-
passed God's purpose in the whole of history and looked for a
liberation of the universe itself. But the church is forever
tempted to limit its expectations to its own members, and
that is a surrender to deadness. So it needs those who have not
forgotten the cries or the marching songs of humanity; and
who better to remind it of them than one who was recently
outside its doors?

So come as pioneers. The aliveness of the church, like that of a shrub-rose, is renewed year by year through the vigorous new shoots that spring from near the base of the tree. They draw their nourishment from the main stock with its taproot and, indeed, it is the stock that gives birth to them. But should these side shoots be regularly cut away the old wood's strength will wane and become unproductive. I am not contrasting new members of the church with those who are long established, but new *ways* of Christian discipleship with more traditional forms. Often it has been an older church member who, after half a lifetime of faithful routine, was moved to initiate some new pattern of expressing love for God and for the world. This was the rationale of the Religious Orders. This is what moved John Wesley to organize lay people of the Established Church in weekly class-meetings, and Count Zinzendorf to set up his *ecclesiolae*, or mini-churches, to enhance the faith of the main Lutheran and Reformed Churches in Central Europe. This too was the strategy of revival through the Oxford Movement. But for every such creative minority that is still remembered there have been scores that were little springs of vitality and challenge in their day and, having played their part, are forgotten.

So when I say, 'Come as pioneers', I am urging you not only to identify yourself with that body of Christians to which it is most natural for you to belong, and to share their worship and work with loyalty, but also to find your place with some of them who, as a group, are committed to a more deliberate and demanding exercise of aliveness. The possibilities are innumerable and you must find your own way. There are groups that are exploring ways of bringing prayer to life. Other groups are looking for a more intimate and supportive quality of fellowship. Sometimes these enterprises are planned on a brief, once-off basis. I recall a six-day pilgrimage walk from Dorchester-on-Thames to Winchester in the course of which seventy-five people of all ages experienced a growth in mutual care and prayer which set a permanent mark on their understanding of Christianity. Tens of thousands have found similar inspiration from a visit to the Taizé Community in France. There are others who have gone further and set up small residential communities where they can pursue together a way of life in which they can remain more fully aware and responsive and withstand the deadening pressures of their secular callings. I know well one such enterprise consisting of two independent communities within a short distance of each other. One shares a large house and garden with the purpose of making it a place of quiet meditation and healing. Its sister community is more active, running workshops and an organic vegetable farm where psychologically disabled people, as well as other guests, can find support and new ideals.

But if in the fellowship of the church the Holy Spirit continues to keep us fully alive and responsive to the pain and need of others, we shall find ourselves in conflict with whatever set-up is causing or perpetuating their plight. A society which is infected with the choice of death rather than life and prefers to be a little blind, a little deaf, will have entrenched that choice in systems of apathy, *laissez-faire* and self-preservation. Those who are awake and aware will at times have either to challenge and resist those systems or collude with them and serve them. This was the test that finally confronted the German Christians under Hitler, and from the spiritual decision that some of them were alive enough to take arose the Confessing Church which spearheaded the revival of the post-war years. Other great issues confront us now. But for the most part the conflict is more local and small-scale and our involvement creeps up on us Christians almost unnoticed until the moment arrives when we either draw back or commit ourselves. This also I have in mind when I say, 'Come as pioneers.' For I have seen in many parts of the world that it is at such points of testing and conflict that a Christian community comes alive to the realities of the gospel most vividly. This is where the distinctiveness of the Christian way of looking at things and of doing things is most clearly recognized. This is where the value of the whole armour of God is proved. It is those who allow their faith to lead them into actual resistance to unjust policies and unscrupulous power-groups who discover that they are 'not wrestling against flesh and blood, but against principalities and powers, against the dark rulers of this world' (Eph. 6.12). George McLeod, who founded the Iona Community and led its work in the Gorbals of Glasgow, said long ago: 'It is only as we Christians commit ourselves in action to the prayer, "Thy Kingdom come on earth", that we truly know how much we need to say "Forgive us", and may literally have to ask for our daily bread because we don't know where it is coming from.'

I end with some lines from a poem by M. Farrow which is also a prayer that gathers up all I have tried to say about this matter of life and death. It is called 'Prayer from the Brink'.

> Give us faces of stone
> To set against the drift,
> To set against the swift, strong, headlong
> Current swollen to a torrent
> That is sweeping our world away . . .
> Give us hearts of flame

To burn against the cold,
To burn against the old, the mortal chill,
The quenching thrill
Of the fast-flooding tide.
Thou art Fire and Light
(Give us hearts of flame!)
Make us to burn like beacons
In defiance of ancient Night.
Make us braziers in the cold streets of the cities,
Make us lamps in Thy sanctuaries,
Make us candles to the Sacred Heart.
The world is lost and is looking for the way.[4]

Father,
forgive us –
By scornful neglect
or by feebly belonging
we have made a dead thing of your church,
crucifying Christ afresh.
Raise us up
to be his Body
in the power of your Spirit,
passionate and free,
open to you,
open to all others,
open to your world.
Amen.

NOTES

Chapter 1   Breath of Life

1. *The Go-Between God*, SCM Press 1972.

2. Martin Buber, *I and Thou*, T. & T. Clark, paperback edn 1966, p. 136.

3. André Maurois, *The Life of Sir Alexander Fleming*, Jonathan Cape 1959, p. 125.

4. Quoted in Edward Robinson, *Living the Questions*, Religious Experience Research Unit, Manchester College, Oxford 1978, pp. 113–14.

5. See Ex. 3.1–10; I Kings 19.11–12.

6. Ms in the archives of the Religious Experience Research Unit.

Chapter 2   More Dead than Alive

1. T. S. Eliot, *Murder in the Cathedral*, Faber 1935, Part I, Second Chorus.

2. T. S. Eliot, *The Hollow Men* from *Poems 1909–1925*, Faber 1925.

3. Ibid.

4. Peter Shaffer, *The Royal Hunt of the Sun*, Penguin 1981, p. 75.

5. Quoted in *God of a Hundred Names* compiled by Barbara Greene and Victor Gollancz, Gollancz 1962, p. 222.

6. C. S. Lewis, *Surprised by Joy*, Geoffrey Bles 1955, p. 211; Fount 1977, p. 179.

Chapter 3   In Him Was Life

1. Dr Elizabeth Kübler-Ross in a broadcast talk published in *The Listener*, 29 September 1983, vol. 110, no. 2828.

2. See Matt. 5.21–22, 27–28, 31–34, 38–39, 43–44.

3. See Mark 3.31–35; Luke 2.48–50; John 2.4.

4. See Luke 9.58; 12.15–21; 7.33–34.

5. See Matt. 5.40; Luke 11.5–6; 5.1–3; 19.28–34.

6. See Mark 5.30; Luke 6.19.

7. Tom Stoppard, *Rosencrantz and Guildenstern are Dead*, Faber 1967, p. 92.

Chapter 4   Resurrection

1. See Xavier Leon-Dufour, *Resurrection and the Message of Easter*, Geoffrey Chapman 1974, p. 43.

2. Michael Ramsey, *Introducing the Christian Faith*, SCM Press 1961, p. 43.

3. Lucas Grollenberg, *Jesus*, SCM Press 1978, p. 1.

4. David Wilkerson, *The Cross and the Switchblade*, Oliphants 1964, p. 161.

5. Thomas Merton, *The Seven-Storey Mountain*, Sheldon Press 1975, pp. 109f.

6. Viktor E. Franke, *Man's Search for Meaning*, Hodder 1962, pp. 89–90.

Chapter 5   The Living God

1. Rosemary Haughton, *The Passionate God*, Darton, Longman & Todd 1981, pp. 18–23.

2. Phil. 4.5.

3. 'Day Dream' from *The Collected Poems of A. S. J. Tessimond* ed Hubert Nicholson, Whiteknight's Press, Reading 1985, p. 48.

4. From *An Anthology of Religious Verse* ed Norman Nicholson, Penguin 1942, p. 86.